COUNTRY INSIGHTS

FRANCE

Teresa Fisher

WAYLAND

COUNTRY INSIGHTS

BRAZIL • CHINA • FRANCE • JAMAICA • JAPAN • KENYA • MEXICO • PAKISTAN

GUIDE TO THIS BOOK

As well as telling you about the whole of France, this book looks closely at the city of Aix-en-Provence and the village of Beuvron-en-Auge.

 This city symbol will appear at the top of the page and information boxes each time the book looks at Aix-en-Provence.

 This rural symbol will appear each time the book looks at Beuvron-en-Auge.

Cover photograph: Two children, aged eleven and twelve, on their way to school in Aix-en-Provence.

Title page: A typical French scene on a café terrace.

Contents page: Picking grapes on a vineyard near Montpellier, in the south of France.

Series and book editor: Polly Goodman
Series and book designer: Tim Mayer
Consultant: Dr. Tony Binns, Geography lecturer and tutor of student teachers at the University of Sussex.

First published in 1996 by
Wayland Publishers Ltd
61 Western Road, Hove
East Sussex, BN3 1JD, England

This paperback edition published in 1999.

© Copyright 1996 Wayland Publishers Ltd

British Library Cataloguing in Publication Data
Fisher, Teresa
　　France. – (Country Insights)
　　1. France – Juvenile literature
　　I. Title
　　944'.0839

PAPERBACK ISBN 0 7502 2523 8

Typeset by Tim Mayer, England

Printed and bound by Eurografica S.p.A , Italy

Contents

Introducing France

France lies at the heart of Western Europe. It is the largest country in Europe, and one of the European Union's largest and most influential countries, playing an important part in world affairs. Its size and central position, bordered by eight different countries, makes it a country of many contrasts and surprises.

Thousands of tourists from all over the world visit France for its beautiful and varied countryside. It is divided into twenty-two regions, including the island of Corsica off the Italian coast. Each region has its own distinctive character and traditions and some even have their own special languages and dialects, such as Breton in Brittany, although French is the official language. France's full name is *La République Française* (The Republic of France), meaning that the entire country is governed by a president, chosen by the French people every seven years. France first became a republic after a peasant uprising in 1789, which started with the capture of the Bastille prison in Paris on 14 July. Today Bastille Day, on 14 July, is a national holiday, with parties, processions and fireworks, and the streets are decorated with the national flag.

French flags in front of the Arc de Triomphe, in Paris. The French flag is called the Tricolore after its colours ('Tri' means 'three' and 'colore' means 'coloured').

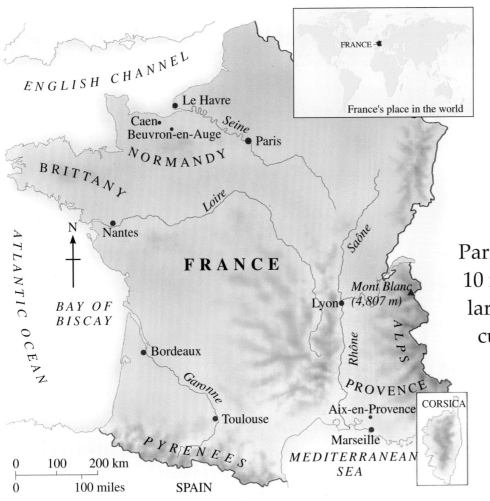

ENGLISH CHANNEL

Le Havre

Caen
Beuvron-en-Auge
Seine
Paris

NORMANDY

BRITTANY

Loire

N

Nantes

FRANCE

Saône

ATLANTIC OCEAN

BAY OF BISCAY

Mont Blanc (4,807 m)
Lyon

ALPS

Rhône

Bordeaux

Garonne

PROVENCE

CORSICA

Toulouse

Aix-en-Provence

Marseille

PYRENEES

MEDITERRANEAN SEA

0   100   200 km

0   100 miles   SPAIN

FRANCE

France's place in the world

This book takes you to the city of Aix-en-Provence and the village of Beuvron-en-Auge, as well as the rest of France. You can find these places on the map.

The French capital, Paris, has a population of 10 million. It is France's largest city and its main cultural and business centre. Other major cities include Lyon, Marseille, Lille and Bordeaux. France is a world leader in industry, famous for its cars, aeroplanes and nuclear power. But it is perhaps better known for its glamorous fashion and perfume, its delicious wine, cheese and, of course, its bubbly champagne.

▼ **The height of fashion: the supermodel Linda Evangelista on a Paris catwalk.**

FRANCE FACTS

Total land area (including Corsica):	**551,670 km^2**
Population:	**57 million**
Capital:	**Paris**
Currency:	**Franc**
Highest mountain:	**Mt Blanc (4,807m)**

All statistic sources are on page 47.

A university city

The ancient city of Aix-en-Provence (pronounced 'Ex-on-Provonce') was once the capital of the Provence region, in southern France. It is located near the popular, Mediterranean seaside resorts of Cannes and St Tropez. The city is very easy to reach, both by train and car, since it lies at the crossroads of the main rail and motorway routes to Italy, Spain and the Alps. It is also just a short distance inland from the large, bustling port of Marseille.

Looking over the old centre of Aix-en-Provence to the new, high-rise development on its outskirts.

Aix was founded by the Romans, around 123 BC, and several Roman remains can still be seen today. The name 'Aix' (which comes from the Latin word 'aquae 'meaning 'water') was given to the city because of its hot mineral springs, where the Romans went to bathe. Many people still visit the springs today to be cured of their aches and pains.

The city layout is typical of many old French cities. Its traffic-free old centre is a maze of tiny, medieval streets, lined with honey-coloured houses, shops, cafés,

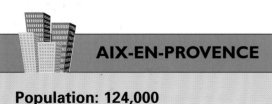

AIX-EN-PROVENCE

Population: 124,000

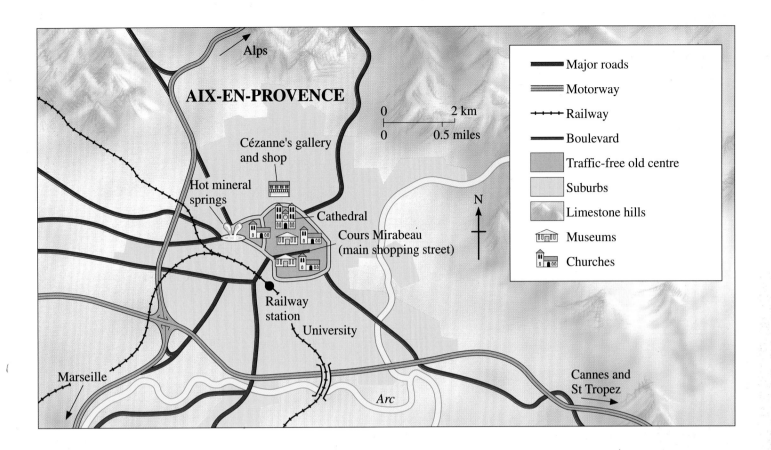

AIX-EN-PROVENCE

Alps

Cézanne's gallery and shop

Hot mineral springs

Cathedral

Cours Mirabeau (main shopping street)

Railway station

University

Marseille

Arc

Cannes and St Tropez

▬▬▬	Major roads
▦▦▦	Motorway
┼┼┼┼	Railway
━━━	Boulevard
■	Traffic-free old centre
▫	Suburbs
▨	Limestone hills
🏛	Museums
⛪	Churches

0   2 km
0   0.5 miles

N

restaurants and peaceful squares. The squares often contain old statues and fountains. The centre is surrounded by a broad, tree-lined boulevard. Newer apartment blocks, offices and parks have all grown outwards from the centre in modern, sprawling suburbs.

There are many students in Aix who attend the university. This large population of young people help to make the city particularly lively, full of bars, discos, theatres, cinemas, concert halls and art galleries.

The city's traffic-free centre is perfect for café terraces like this one, named **Le Cézanne,** *after the famous artist who lived in the city.*

7

Picture-postcard village

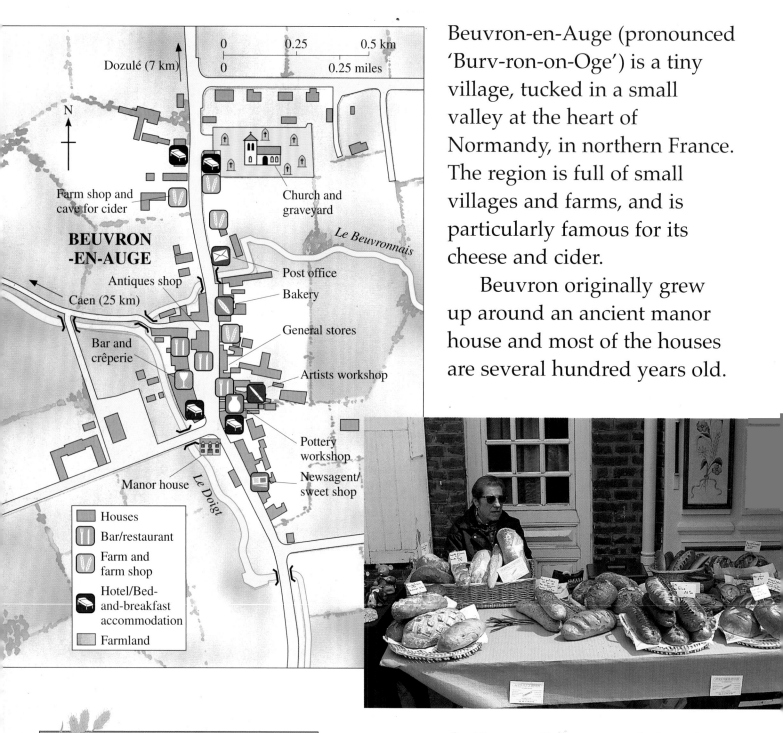

Beuvron-en-Auge (pronounced 'Burv-ron-on-Oge') is a tiny village, tucked in a small valley at the heart of Normandy, in northern France. The region is full of small villages and farms, and is particularly famous for its cheese and cider.

Beuvron originally grew up around an ancient manor house and most of the houses are several hundred years old.

A villager sells home-made bread outside her house. Home-made goods sell well to tourists who visit the village.

BEUVRON-EN-AUGE

Population: 274

Map labels:
- Dozulé (7 km)
- 0   0.25   0.5 km
- 0   0.25 miles
- N
- Farm shop and cave for cider
- Church and graveyard
- BEUVRON -EN-AUGE
- Le Beuvronnais
- Antiques shop
- Post office
- Caen (25 km)
- Bakery
- General stores
- Bar and crêperie
- Artists workshop
- Pottery workshop
- Manor house
- Le Doigt
- Newsagent/ sweet shop

Legend:
- Houses
- Bar/restaurant
- Farm and farm shop
- Hotel/Bed-and-breakfast accommodation
- Farmland

All the houses are made of brick with wooden timbers and painted different colours. At the centre of the village is the old market square, surrounded by a few essential shops (a baker, newsagent and a general stores), as well as several craft shops, a café and restaurants for visitors. There is also a village church, which holds one service a week on Sunday mornings.

Otherwise, facilities in the village are extremely limited. There are no banks, doctors or sports facilities and even the village school closed down recently. The nearest town, Dozulé, is just over 7 kilometres away, but there is no public transport.

However, the people of Beuvron enjoy a slower, healthier and more peaceful lifestyle than city people. This is why a quarter of the French population choose to live in the countryside, in small villages like Beuvron-en-Auge, rather than in towns and cities.

'We are very proud of our village, which is considered to be one of the most beautiful villages in France, and we work hard to keep it neat and tidy.' – Pascal Fouquet, farmer.

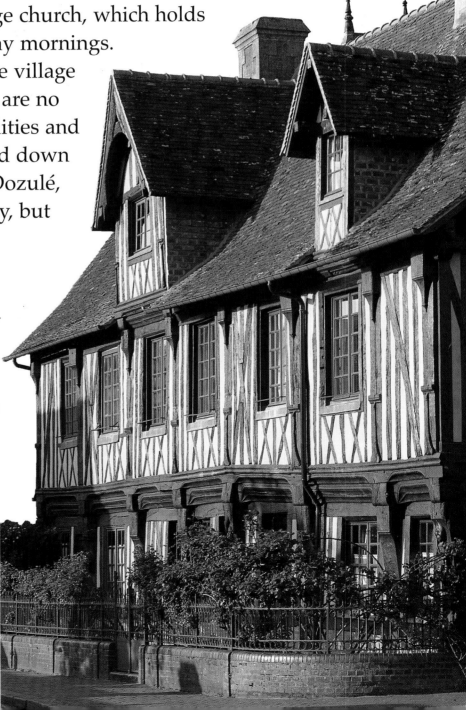

This is the ancient manor house which the village first grew around, hundreds of years ago.

Landscape and climate

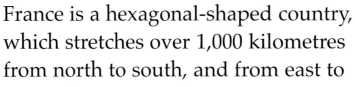

France is a hexagonal-shaped country, which stretches over 1,000 kilometres from north to south, and from east to west. The countryside varies greatly from region to region, from fertile farmland in the north, west and south-west, to the snow-capped peaks of the Pyrénées and the Alps mountain ranges. Between these two mountain ranges, the southern coastline of France is washed by the warm Mediterranean Sea, with its popular sandy beaches.

The northern coastline is more rugged, particularly in Brittany, where small, rocky bays face the stormy Atlantic Ocean. Inland France is mostly meadows and woodland. Forests cover about a quarter of the country, which means that timber is an important natural resource. France has more farmland than any other country in Europe. The main crops grown are wheat, barley, grapes and apples.

Much of France's northern coastline is wild and remote.

▲ *Skiers trekking in the Pyrénées mountains, on the border with Spain.*

FRANCE'S CLIMATE	
Average summer temperatures:	North: 19 ˚C
	South: 24 ˚C
Average winter temperatures:	North: 3 ˚C
	South: 9 ˚C
	Alps: –0 ˚C

▼ *Grapes are picked and collected in a trailer, to be made into wine.*

France also has contrasts in climate. The north, west and south-west usually have cool summers and mild winters with frequent rain, while the mountainous regions in the east have warm summers and cold winters with lots of snow. The south coast has little rain, warm winters and hot, dry summers. This varying climate, combined with the physical features of the countryside, dictates where most people live. Many people live in the south due to the milder climate, while very few people live in the mountain regions. Most of the larger towns and cities are located near the coast or alongside the Rhône, the Seine, the Loire or the Garonne, France's four main rivers.

Sun-baked city

Aix-en-Provence lies 25 kilometres inland from the Mediterranean Sea. To the west lies the important River Rhône, which flows across a wide, flat valley of marshy lakes and lagoons. France's largest lake, the Etang de Berre, to the west of the city, is lined with modern industries.

From the city limits you can see the limestone hills around Aix-en-Provence.

On three sides of the city there are limestone hills, with a variety of vegetation from barren, dusty scrubland to thick, pine forests. To the north is a popular region for walkers and nature lovers, where wild boars, rare eagles and owls can still be seen. To the east lie the rugged hills of the Saint-Victoire mountain range.

Aix-en-Provence has a Mediterranean climate, with long, hot summers, very little rain and lots of sunshine. Spring and autumn are the wettest seasons, and winters are usually warm and dry. There is, however, a strong, icy wind, called the *mistral,* which is feared by many French people. In winter and early spring, the *mistral* can destroy crops and blow down trees and buildings.

Many trees and flowers grow in and around the city because the climate is sunny and mild. Olive groves, fruit trees (lemons, peaches, cherries and apricots) and lavender fields make a colourful landscape and many of the gently sloping hillsides are covered in rows of vines for making wine. Provence produces more flowers than anywhere in France, many of which are made into perfume. Other local specialities are sweet-smelling herbs (sage, thyme and rosemary) and truffles. These are black, savoury, golf-ball-sized delicacies, sniffed out of the earth by pigs on leads, and then sold for high prices in the local markets.

PAUL CÉZANNE

The famous artist Paul Cézanne (1839–1906) lived in Aix-en-Provence for most of his life. He loved painting the landscapes around the city. Cézanne's favourite subject was the dramatic Saint-Victoire mountain, the highest peak in the area, which he painted over sixty-five times. Today, Cézanne's paintings are great collectors' pieces, and as a result, the mountain is famous all over the world.

◀ **Olives grown locally are sold in the city's markets.**

▲ **Cézanne's shop and museum is just one of the tourist attractions in the city.**

A cool northern valley

Beuvron lies at the centre of the fertile Pays d'Auge region. *'Pays d'Auge'* means 'countryside of troughs' (or valleys). Beuvron-en-Auge got its name because the village is hidden in a small valley. All around are rolling hills mixed with thick woodland and a maze of small rivers and streams, two of which flow right through the village. Everywhere you look there are lush, green pastures, neatly divided by hedges on either side of narrow lanes that wind through the countryside.

In the spring, the hedgerows are spotted with purple orchids and yellow primroses, and the fruit trees in the orchards are covered in pink blossom. By the autumn, the red and golden fruit are ready for picking and the air is full of the sweet smell of ripe apples and pears.

The village has a mild climate all year round, with cool, wet winters and warm summers. Besides apples and pears, which are made into cider, and Calvados (an apple brandy), the other main crops around the village are corn, wheat, beetroot, peas and potatoes. This is one of France's main dairy-farming regions, well-known for its large, brown-and-cream cows which can be seen grazing in the meadows.

> **'We are very lucky with our mild climate here because it is perfect for all types of farming.'** – Annette Fouquet, farmer.

A farmer feeds her chickens in one of the village's farmyards. You can see the brown-and-cream, Normandy cows in the background.

14

The Beuvronnais river winds through the village.

Home life

Family life is very important to the French and the average family spends a lot of time together. Children often stay up late in the evenings, talking over dinner, or reading or watching television with their parents. They are also expected to help around the house with laying the table, tidying their rooms and other housework. At weekends, the whole family will often go out for the day or enjoy sporting activities together. Cycling is a particularly popular family pastime.

When teenagers grow up and leave school, they tend to live at home longer than in many Western countries, often not having their own home until they have been working for several years or until they get married.

Mealtimes are family occasions in France. This is Sunday lunch in a farmhouse in the Ardèche region, in the south of France.

FRENCH MEALS

For breakfast, the French usually eat part of a baguette (a long, thin, loaf of bread) and drink a bowl of coffee or hot chocolate. At lunch and supper, vegetables and salad always come after the main fish or meat course, and cheese comes before the pudding. Bread is placed in a basket or bowl on the table. Before starting to eat in France, it is polite to say *'Bon appetit'*, which means 'enjoy your meal'.

▲ **Apartment blocks are home for many French people.**

There are many different types of home in France. In villages, most people live in houses with gardens. But three-quarters of the French population live in towns and cities, where almost everyone lives in apartments. These range from smart, spacious, luxury flats for wealthy families, to high-rise council flats on the sprawling outskirts of large cities. The council flats are mainly for families who are unemployed or who have poorly paid jobs.

The French love their food and wine, and France is well-known for its delicious cooking. Meals usually consist of a number of courses and can last for several hours. Some well-known French delicacies are *escargots* (snails served hot with garlic butter), grilled frogs legs, pâté and crêpes (pancakes). Most families, including the children, drink wine at mealtimes, sometimes mixed with water.

▼ **A selection of French cheeses and meats on a market stall.**

Apartment homes

The open shutters of a town house, in a square in the old centre of Aix.

Most people in Aix live in rented apartments, usually in a block of flats with a caretaker. Some very rich families live in the city centre in old town houses with shady courtyards. Most homes in this part of the city also have brightly coloured wooden shutters, which keep them warm in winter and cool in summer. Increasingly, however, families are moving away from the hustle and bustle of the city centre, to live in the rapidly expanding, new suburbs.

Nine-year-old Michelle Bertrand's family have recently moved from the countryside into a flat in Aix, on the top floor of a six-storey apartment block. It has three bedrooms, a large living room, kitchen, bathroom and a sunny balcony. Many families in Aix have two cars, two televisions and, like Michelle's family, a computer.

POPULATION DENSITY

Aix-en-Provence: 667 people per km²

'I like living in the city but I really miss playing in the garden. My family have recently bought a computer, so I guess I can play with that now instead.' – Michelle Bertrand, 9 years old.

Children in Aix generally spend less time at home with their families than village children, because the city offers so many other activities, such as sports clubs and scout groups. However, family activities are also important and most weekends, the whole family will eat out together at one of the city's many restaurants.

▲ *Shopping at the hypermarket on the city outskirts.*

At weekends, Michelle's family goes to the giant hypermarket on the city outskirts, where they can buy everything from milk to mountain bikes. The city centre is always busy with people shopping, especially in the car-free city centre, with its fashionable boutiques, small specialist stores and colourful fruit, vegetable and flower markets.

▼ *The daily vegetable market in the centre of the city.*

Home life in Beuvron-en-Auge

A grandparent looks out of a house in the village, which has a window in the door that can open and close.

Most people in Beuvron live in a house with a garden, which they own. Grandparents often live with their families. Since the village is such a small community, everyone knows and helps one another.

Although most families have a car, a telephone and a television, many, like the Fouquet family, do not have many of the modern luxuries found in the cities, such as a computer, dish-washer or microwave. Shopping facilities are also limited. The village stores sell essentials such as milk, bread and meat, but if the Fouquet's shopping list is longer, they have to drive to the local towns of Dozulé or Caen.

Children in the village are expected to help with household chores and preparing the meals more than city children. The kitchen is the most important room in the house for the Fouquet family.

POPULATION DENSITY
Beuvron-en-Auge: 275 people per km²

It is here that they gather on Sundays for a huge lunch, often with four or five courses, usually lasting all afternoon. Their friends are invited as well, often bringing home-made cakes with them. Everyone is proud of their food and cooking in the village, which is full of local ingredients, especially cream, cider and apples.

▲ *Villagers have to drive to Dozulé or Caen to buy anything more than basic foods.*

▼ *The village* **boulangerie** *(bakery).*

France at work

Along with the USA, Germany and Japan, France is one of the world's leading exporters of manufactured goods, and its manufacturing industries employ thousands of people. These industries use the latest technologies. Many of their products are world famous, including cars made by Renault, Peugeot and Citroën, Michelin tyres and TGV trains, the fastest trains in the world.

The type of work differs between the various regions, from manufacturing work in busy industrial areas, to farming in the countryside. In the Alps and coastal areas, tourism is the major industry, with many people working in hotels and restaurants.

France's manufacturing industries are mostly centred around the rivers and ports, and include aircraft, car and ship-building. Many traditional industries and types of agriculture still exist, including fishing in Brittany, perfume in Provence, and champagne, which comes from an area near Paris called Champagne.

Crates of apples are filled in Limousin, a region in central France. Apples are a major crop in France, and they are sold all over the world.

Paris is not only France's capital city, but also its political, financial, commercial and cultural centre, with over half the country's business based there. It is also one of the leading fashion centres of the world.

France is an important farming country. The northern and central areas are particularly suited to cereals and livestock, while the sunny south is ideal for fruit, especially oranges, lemons, peaches, apricots and grapes. The grapes are made into red, white and rosé wines, which are then shipped worldwide. France supplies a quarter of all the world's wine, and it is the country's most famous product.

▲ *Most factories in France keep working through the night.*

A waiter on a restaurant ▶ terrace. France's restaurants, cafés and hotels provide many jobs in the catering industry.

TYPE OF WORK IN FRANCE	
	Percentage of population
Services:	65
Manufacturing:	29
Agriculture:	6

Business and industries

Most people in Aix work in the many banks, solicitors' and commercial offices in the city centre, or in the big industrial parks and factories outside the city. Tourism is important too, and a large number of people work in the city's hotels, restaurants, galleries and museums.

Henri Dupont, a solicitor, lives on the outskirts of Aix. He commutes by bus each day to his office in the city centre. His neighbour, Jean Michel, is a scientist who drives to work at the giant, high-tech Cadarache Centre for Nuclear Research, just beyond the city. Many commuters head out of Aix by car or train to the surrounding factories. It is only 25 kilometres to Marseille, France's most important port and ship-building centre, and less than half an hour's drive to the Etang de Berre, one of France's main industrial areas. Here there are oil, natural gas and petrochemical industries and Europe's largest helicopter factory.

Bank workers in the city centre. Aix is a major business centre so most people work in offices.

'These days I have to leave my car behind and go to work by bus. The traffic jams in the city centre seem to get worse every year.' – Nicole Massip, bank manager.

▲ *The Citroën car sales centre on the outskirts of Aix. Car sales are big business in the city.*

Traditional local industries also exist in the city. Many people work in small factories making Provençal products such as canned fruits, jam, and brightly patterned fabrics. In the colourful, daily markets in the city centre, market traders sell locally grown fruit, flowers and vegetables, as well as excellent red, white and rosé wines. Aix is also an important sweet-manufacturing centre, producing diamond-shaped marzipan sweets, called *Calissons*, and chocolates from the famous Puyricard factory, on the northern outskirts of the city.

▼ *Traditional Provençal cloth is sold in the city centre.*

Cider, cheeses and horses

There are no large industries in Beuvron-en-Auge, only small, family-run businesses based on farming, country crafts and traditions. The village's region has a long tradition in horse-breeding, and one of the farms breeds and trains racehorses.

Beuvron is one of a group of cider-producing villages clustered around the market town of Cambremer. Jacques Duval has orchards here and still makes his cider using old-fashioned, heavy wooden presses. He also produces a strong, alcoholic drink called *Calvados*, and a sherry-like drink called *pommeau*, both made out of apples. Every spring, Jacques takes samples of these drinks to Cambremer to be graded. The best drinks are given a special award, called the *Cru de Cambremer*.

Apart from cider, Beuvron also produces three types of cheese, including *Camembert*. Have you ever eaten some *Camembert* or seen it in the

'If I win the *Cru de Cambremer* award this year I'll be allowed to place a special sign outside my farm which means that passers-by will hopefully buy some cider.' – Jacques Duval, cider producer.

Jacques Duval checks his cider.

supermarket? It is mild and creamy, with quite a strong smell, and is packed in small, round, wooden boxes. Two other village cheeses – the large *Pavé d'Auge* (*'pavé'* means 'paving stone') and a small, round *Beuvronnais* – are made by hand in the village and sold in the village stores.

Although there are only a few shops in Beuvron, several artists and potters have recently opened studios in the village. The wooden, covered market hall also contains a few small antique shops. All the shops close over lunchtime so that families can be together for their midday meal.

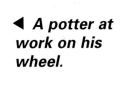

▲ Racehorses are trained at the village stud.

▼ Boxes of Pavé d'Auge cheese, made in the village by hand.

◄ A potter at work on his wheel.

Going to school

The education system in France is carefully planned by the government and is the same throughout the country. Most schools are free (state schools) although there are a few private schools, mostly run by the Catholic Church. Children do not have to wear a uniform and they have long holidays, including a two-and-a-half-month summer break, but they usually have lots of homework to do during this time! Many children start school as young as two or three years old in a nursery school, or *école maternelle*, but they do not have to start until primary school, at the age of six. When they are eleven years old, children move on to a secondary school for another five years.

A typical school day starts at 8.30 am and ends at 4.30 pm, with a two-hour lunchbreak, although some secondary schools have slightly longer days. Most schools have classes on Saturday mornings, but Wednesday afternoons are free for children to play sport, or join in activities such as painting, drama or dance at the local youth club.

Most children eat in the school canteen, unless they live close enough to go home for lunch.

SCHOOL IN FRANCE

Average number of pupils per class:	**25–30**
Average length of lessons:	**55 minutes**
Average amount of homework:	**1–2 hours a night**
Pupils who go to university:	**60 per cent**

The official school-leaving age is sixteen. But many children continue for two more years at a technical college, a trade school, or if they want to go to university, a *lycée* school. *Lycée* schools give a more general education that leads to an exam in several subjects, called *Le Baccalauréat*, which is recognized worldwide.

▼ *Football is the most popular sport for schoolchildren in France.*

▼ *Secondary school children working on a team project together.*

School in the city

'My favourite subject at school is science and technology. When I'm older I want to go to university here and then become a computer expert.' – Michelle Bertrand, 9 years old.

There is a large choice of schools for children in Aix, with about sixty state schools and over twenty private schools. Many children are dropped off at school by their parents on their way to work, otherwise they catch the bus. Michelle Bertrand goes by school bus because it goes past her street, but many of Michelle's friends, who live further away, use public transport.

Schools in Aix are quite large, often with over 500 pupils, and have good facilities. Some schools have their own playing fields, but others use the city's superb sports grounds. All children take part in sports, including athletics, gymnastics and team sports such as football, volleyball and basketball. Most schools have computers since computer studies

Computer studies are taught in most schools in France.

is part of the timetable, and many children are able to practise at home on their parents' computer.

Sometimes schools, especially primary schools, organize a study 'holiday' during term-time. Michelle's favourite is a *classe de neige* (snow class), when the whole class spends a week at a nearby ski resort like Grenoble. But she also enjoys the *classe de mer* by the seaside. During the week the children still have lessons, but it is always more fun than at school itself.

There are more job opportunities for children in Aix than for those in the villages because there are so many different companies and types of work in the city. Academic qualifications are very important for these jobs, so many children go to the university in the city. The university in Aix is considered to be one of the best in the country.

School in Beuvron-en-Auge

▲ *The school bus stops in the village every day to take children to school in Dozulé.*

Since many families have moved out of Beuvron in the last few years to nearby towns, where there are better jobs, there are fewer children left in the village. As a result, the village school had to close at the end of 1995, so all the children now go to school in the nearby town of Dozulé.

Jean-Philippe Fouquet and his sister Marie Fouquet, have to get up very early each morning to catch the school bus, which takes about 15 minutes. Jean-Philippe's bus arrives at 7.30 am to take him to the secondary school, while Marie, who attends the primary school, leaves at 8.30 am. Sometimes Jean-Philippe gets up even earlier so that he can help his father milk the cows.

Dozulé is a small town, and there are only four schools: a nursery school, a primary school and a secondary school which are free, and one private school. All the schools are quite small, with about 300 children in each, and facilities are limited.

◄ *The end of the school day at the primary school in Dozulé.*

All the schools share the same sports ground, but they each have a playground with swings, slides and climbing frames. In their lunchbreak, the children play games such as hopskotch and skipping.

Each school has a canteen where the children eat lunch. Jean-Philippe really likes the school food and enjoys playing football with his friends. Marie wishes she could go home for lunch like her friends who live in Dozulé, but she has to wait until the end of the day before the school bus can take her home to Beuvron.

'A few of my friends want to go to university when they finish school and then get a job in a big city like Paris. I don't though because I'm going to take over my father's farm when I grow up.' – Jean-Philippe Fouquet, 11 years old.

'Cat's cradle' and skipping are favourite games played at lunchtime in the playground.

33

France at play

Leisure time is very important to the French. In the towns and cities, people spend half their spare time either reading or going to the cinema, theatre or concerts. The world's first cinema opened in Paris in 1895. Children play in parks, go to friends' houses, watch television, or read popular comics such as *Asterix* or *Tintin*. The most popular hobbies at the moment are Rollerblading and computer games.

French people love sport and there are clubs in every town and in many villages. The most popular sport is football, followed by cycling, swimming, sailing and rugby.

▲ **Most French children learn to ski from the age of three.**

▲ **A Rollerblader jumps off a specially designed pipe.**

The world's longest and most famous cycling race is the French *Tour de France*, with thousands of cyclists competing over three weeks in the summer. Another big race is the twenty-four-hour *Le Mans* car race. Tennis is popular and one of the world's top tournaments is held in Paris every spring. There are also some traditional sports that are only found in certain regions, such as bull running in the Camargue, and *pelota* (which is similar to squash) in the Basque region near Spain.

The French usually have six weeks' holiday a year, including a month's holiday in July or August. Most people prefer to stay in France for their holidays than go abroad. In winter, people travel from all over the country to the Alps for skiing. In summer, they enjoy hiking, canoeing and climbing, or head south to the Rivière, France's most popular holiday destination.

The traditional sport of bull running through the streets of Nîmes, in the south of France.

Leisure in Aix-en-Provence

Aix has a wide range of leisure activities. There are lots of sports clubs, public swimming pools and parks to play in, or museums, libraries and galleries to visit. Many children are members of scout groups and there are also several youth clubs which organize parties, games and outings to places of interest near the city.

Everyone likes dining out in Aix. Many cafés are open from early morning to late at night. In the summer, chairs and tables spill out on to the pavements, where people meet to chat, drink coffee, read the newspapers or just watch the world go by.

While Michelle Bertrand and her mother are out shopping, her father enjoys a game of boule in a shady square. This is a traditional French game, where players throw heavy, metal balls, trying to get closest to a small, wooden ball called a *cochonnet* (meaning 'piglet'!)

'I often go camping with my family in the summer. It's great fun because there are always lots of children to play with and I'm allowed to go to bed later than normal.' – Michelle Bertrand, 9 years old.

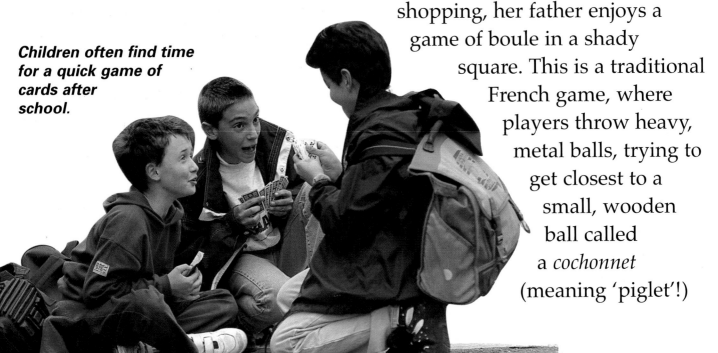

Children often find time for a quick game of cards after school.

A game of boule in a square in the city centre.

In the evenings there are jazz bars, nightclubs, discos and a casino. There is always plenty of entertainment at the city theatres and concert halls, including a world-famous music festival in August.

At weekends, many people leave the city. The surrounding hilly countryside is good for hiking, horse-riding and mountain-biking. In winter, it only takes three hours by car to reach Grenoble, the nearest major ski resort. Michelle enjoys summer weekends best because she often goes camping with her parents, or stays with her friend's family in their weekend seaside home near the popular resort of St Tropez.

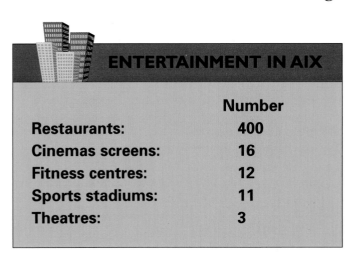

ENTERTAINMENT IN AIX	
	Number
Restaurants:	400
Cinemas screens:	16
Fitness centres:	12
Sports stadiums:	11
Theatres:	3

Leisure time in Beuvron -en-Auge

ENTERTAINMENT IN BEUVRON	
	Number
Restaurants:	3
Cafés:	1

Computer games are popular among both village and city children.

There is much less choice of activities and sports in Beuvron than in Aix because there are no sports or youth clubs. So children have to find other ways of amusing themselves, such as playing football in the fields, paddling in the river or messing about on bikes. After school, when they have finished their homework, most children are allowed to watch television. Jean-Philippe and his sister Marie like quiz shows and cartoons best. At weekends they spend most of the time outdoors together with their parents on long, country walks or cycle rides.

There are several sports clubs in the surrounding villages, such as tennis, golf and horse-riding, but joining them is expensive. Fishing, hunting and shooting are also very popular for adults. The sea is only a short drive away for swimming, sailing, windsurfing and playing on the beach. On Wednesday afternoons and also during the school holidays, most children go to the *centre de jeunesse* (youth club) at Dozulé, where there is always a busy programme of sports events, dancing, singing and painting.

▲ *The many small rivers and streams near the village are good fun for children to play in.*

The villagers of Beuvron are very proud of their traditional way of life and they have preserved old costumes, dances, arts and crafts. Each month there is usually a special event in the village. There is a geranium fair in the spring, craft displays, a jam-making competition and a music festival during the summer, a large, traditional market in the autumn, and a Christmas market to end the year.

'The youth centre is really brilliant because sometimes we go on trips to the local aquarium, the swimming pool, or in summer, to the seaside.' – Marie Fouquet, 8 years old.

◀ *The geranium festival in the spring fills the village streets with flower displays and tourists.*

The future

France will continue to play an important part in the world in the future. As a key member of the European Union, it is pushing for European countries to work closer together and to use the same currency, to increase Europe's wealth.

But France has problems to face, too, particularly unemployment and racism. As people have moved away from villages to cities in search of work, many cities have doubled in size, and there is greater competition for jobs. This has caused increasing racism towards the large numbers of immigrants who have moved to France, hoping for work and a better life.

However, France continues to be a world leader in industry and agriculture, especially heavy industry, telecommunications and alternative energy. The country's successful nuclear industry provides one-third of its electricity and it is the fourth-largest exporter in the world of both manufactured and agricultural products. France has the fastest trains in the world (TGVs), and the recently completed Channel Tunnel now links up with England, 50 kilometres under the English Channel.

A worker in France's electronic industry.

The Channel Tunnel should help France continue to be one of the world's most popular tourist destinations, attracting visitors from all over the world to its summer and winter resorts.

Electricians from France's national electric board (EDF) repair some cables.

41

A prosperous future

New building sites on the city outskirts. Aix is growing as new businesses are attracted to the wealthy city.

The population of Aix has tripled over the last fifty years, as people have moved to the city from the countryside to find work. New suburbs and factories have been built, especially in the fast-growing, high-tech and research industries, which have created jobs and kept unemployment low. There are plans for a large, electronic industrial zone, called Europôle, just south of the city. A new high-speed train line is also planned, which will link the city with Paris by TGV in under three hours.

Aix does not suffer from the pollution of other large, industrial cities because its industries are mainly high-tech, so they do not burn large amounts of fuel. Industry is also restricted to the outskirts of the city, keeping the centre for offices and shops. The traffic-free centre keeps traffic pollution low. This means it is attractive to tourists, whose numbers have increased over the past few years. So even though Aix is now a major business centre, it is still a pleasant place to visit.

Aix has also become a stylish, modern city thanks to its active student population.

'Although we realize we can't stop progress, we are anxious to preserve our pedestrian city centre and to continue to welcome tourists to our city.' – Bernard Martin, restauranteur.

POPULATION GROWTH IN AIX, 1946–96	
1946	46,053
1996	124,000

The city continues to be one of France's most important cultural centres, attracting the world's best musicians and singers to perform there, and is often nicknamed the 'Paris of the South'. As a result, the cost of living and, in particular, house prices have increased enormously over the last few years. But the city's sunny climate and location near the seaside and mountains make it a very popular place to live. As the city expands, the people of Aix-en-Provence can look forward to a prosperous future.

The city's climate and traffic-free centre makes it an ideal tourist spot.

The future of Beuvron -en-Auge

These girls will probably move away from the village when they leave school, to find work in the cities of Paris or Caen.

The population of Beuvron has fallen over the last fifty years, as young people have moved away to the towns and cities in search of work. As a result, the population of the village is getting older and there are increasingly fewer children in the village.

The number of farm workers has also decreased dramatically, with fewer people interested in a career in farming. This is a trend that can be seen all over France. In recent years, the traditional pattern of farming has changed considerably. Many small, family farms have given way to large-scale, high-tech farming. Most of the cheese in Normandy is now factory-made instead of being made by hand. Even cider, one of the region's main products, is mostly produced in factories today. Hand-made produce from small, family farms cannot compete with the amount produced by factories, so the villagers are aware that they will have to find an alternative future for Beuvron other than small-scale farming.

POPULATION IN BEUVRON-EN-AUGE, 1946–96	
1946	411
1996	274

▲ *Tourists enjoy a drink at the village café.*

Fortunately, Beuvron is registered as one of the most beautiful villages in France, so the villagers are encouraging tourism as much as possible. More families are now offering bed-and-breakfast accommodation in their homes, and there are already numerous craft shops, a café, bar, two restaurants, a crêperie and picturesque houses, which attract lots of tourists to the village each year.

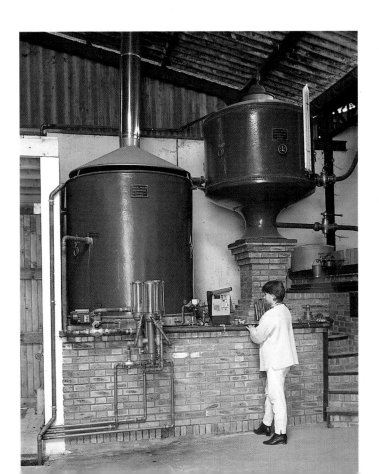

'We are all sad that the young are leaving our beautiful village. But in some parts of France, the young want to live in the country and work in the towns. Perhaps it will happen here too?' – Pascal Fouquet, farmer.

◀ *Increasingly, cider is being produced in factories like this one on the village outskirts, rather than on farms.*

Glossary

alternative energy Energy produced from natural sources, such as falling water (hydroelectricity) or the sun (solar power).

boulevard A wide, usually tree-lined, road in a city.

commercial The purchase and sale of goods.

commute To travel some distance to get to work.

council flats Apartments provided by the government, often for people with low incomes.

crêperie A restaurant that specializes in crêpes (pancakes).

cultural Anything to do with artistic activities (such as theatre, art, dance and museums).

currency The money used by a country (for example the British pound, the French franc and the Japanese yen).

European Union (EU) A group of fifteen European countries, made up of France, Germany, Britain, Italy, Denmark, Ireland, Sweden, Finland, Austria, Spain, Portugal, Greece, the Netherlands, Belguim and Luxemburg, who are working together for the interests of Europe.

exporter Seller of goods to foreign countries.

financial Anything to do with money.

heavy industry Industry producing goods such as metal and machinery.

high-tech industries Industries specializing in complicated technology, for example, computers.

hypermarket A very large supermarket.

lagoons Shallow ponds connected with the sea.

livestock Animals, such as cows and sheep, which are raised on a farm.

manor house A large country house, originally lived in by a lord.

natural resource A natural material (such as coal and water) that can be used by man.

peasant A poor person.

political Relating to the state or government.

population density The number of people living in an area of land.

prosperous Successful.

racism The dislike of a person or people because of their race.

republic A country without a royal family, which usually has a president, who is voted by the people as its head of state.

scrubland An area of poor soil and little vegetation.

service industries Companies which provide a service rather that a product (for example banking and entertainment).

suburbs Districts on the edge of a large town or city.

telecommunications The high-tech industry that deals with communication over a distance, such as by telephone or fax.

unemployment Without work.

Further information

Books to Read

Focus on France and the French by Anita Ganeri (Aladdin, 1995)

Our Country: France by Julia Powell (Wayland, 1990)

Modern Industrial World: France by Mick Dunford (Wayland, 1994)

Country Fact File: France by Bussolin (Simon and Schuster Young Books, 1994)

Usborne First Book of France by L. Somerville (Usborne, 1993)

Getting To Know: France and the French by Nicola Wright (Franklin Watts, 1992)

Look Inside: France by Ian James and Joy Richardson (Franklin Watts, 1995)

The Lands and Peoples of France by Ed Needham (Franklin Watts, 1995)

Fiction:
Château Mystère: A French Puzzle Story by Kathy Gemmell and Susannah Leigh (Usborne, 1994)

Useful Addresses

Maison de la France (French Government Tourist Office), 178 Piccadilly, London W1V 0AL Tel: 0891 244123 provides tourist information on all areas of France.

France House, Digbith Street, Stow-on-the-Wold, Gloucestershire GL54 1BN Tel: 01451 870871 have a wide selection of books tapes, videos, posters and maps of France.

Cultural Section, French Embassy, 23 Cromwell Road, London SW7 2EL Tel: 0171 838 2055

SOURCES

Aix-en-Provence Tourist Office; *Annual Abstract of Statistics* (*Institute Nationale de la Statistiques*, 1995); Bournemouth University; *Encyclopedia Britannica*; *Mairie de la Beuvron-en-Auge*; INSEE Haute-Normandie; *Maison de la France* (French Government Tourist Office), London; *Philips Geographical Digest, 1996–97* (Heinemann, 1996).

PICTURE ACKNOWLEDGEMENTS

All photographs, except the ones listed below, are by James Morris and Dorian Shaw of Axiom Photographic Agency. Page 5: Andrew Lamb © The Conde Nast PL/Vogue; page 16: Wayland Picture Library (Chris Fairclough); page 35: Tony Stone Worldwide (Mark Junak). Map artwork: page 5: Peter Bull; pages 7 and 8: Hardlines.

Index

Page numbers in **bold** refer to photographs.